# 101 Surprising Facts

ABOUT ST. PETER'S AND THE

# VATICAN

Cover and interior design by Caroline Kiser

Photos copyright © Justin Gaeta unless otherwise noted in image credits

Cataloging-in-Publication data on file with the Library of Congress

ISBN: 978-1-61890-687-8

Published in the United States by
Saint Benedict Press, LLC
PO Box 410487
Charlotte, NC 28241
www.SaintBenedictPress.com

Printed and bound in the United States of America

# 101 Surprising FACTS

## ABOUT ST. PETER'S AND THE

# VATICAN

## FR. JEFFREY KIRBY, S.T.L.

WITH ORIGINAL PHOTOGRAPHS FROM JUSTIN AND CHALLISS GAETA

To the Priests and
Seminarians of the
Pontifical North
American College
Vatican City State

# Foreword

Jesus Christ is the center of the Catholic faith, as St. Peter the Apostle boldly proclaimed in Jerusalem 2,000 year ago: "There is salvation in no one else, for there is no other name under heaven given among men by which we must be saved" (Acts 4:12).

It is not surprising then that, when one approaches the monumental setting of St. Peter's Square and Basilica in Rome, this truth is grandly displayed. On the center top of the external façade of the basilica, there stands a giant statue of the Risen Lord Jesus, triumphant and holding the Cross on which he saved humanity, his hand lifted in blessing over all who enter this largest church in the world. In the center of the great square stands the 135-foot obelisk on which is carved the words: "Christ conquers, Christ reigns, Christ rules."

Only in the spirit of deep Christian faith can one truly appreciate the awesome structure that is St. Peter's Basilica. Peter himself was Jesus' chief disciple, the one to whom the Lord entrusted the continuation of his own mission—"I tell you, you are the 'Rock' (*petras*), and on this rock I will build my church

and the gates of hell shall not prevail against it" (Matthew 16:18).

Peter courageously took up his mission, as his first sermon in Jerusalem bears witness. He fulfilled Jesus' command to him: "Strengthen your brethren" (cf. Luke 22:32). Eventually Peter came to Rome where there was already a strong Jewish community to whom he could first announce the fulfillment of their hopes in the person of the Messiah, Jesus of Nazareth.

It seems that this early Jewish-Christian community became a scapegoat used by the Emperor Nero to deflect blame for the disastrous fire which destroyed much of Rome in 64 AD. Jews and Christians were cruelly tortured and Peter himself was crucified (upside down, at his request) in the area of the Vatican Hill. The early Christians took his relics and interred them in the existing necropolis on the Vatican Hill. A Roman priest, Gaius, put up a small wall shrine to protect the relics.

When, after centuries of persecution, Christianity became legalized in 313 AD by Constantine, the Emperor wished to erect a fitting monument to St. Peter. The Emperor

leveled the Vatican Hill at the exact spot of Peter's shrine and built a worthy church over it.

This first St. Peter's Basilica understandably became a major center of worship and pilgrimage for Christians all over Europe. From the time of Pope St. Gregory the Great (590–604 AD), there has been an uninterrupted group of praying clergy at the basilica. In 1053 AD, Pope Leo IX created an Archpriest and a body of Canons—priests who would be responsible for divine worship on a stable basis. This group has continued this privileged task for about a thousand years. In 2013, I was humbled to be named to this Chapter of Canons by Pope Benedict XVI—the only American serving in this capacity.

In 1506 AD, Pope Julius II decided to replace the Constantinian Basilica, which by his time was in disrepair and collapsing. The pope employed the greatest Renaissance geniuses—Michelangelo, Raphael, Bramante, and Bernini—to build a worthy replacement. The new basilica became the greatest Church in Christendom and a visible sign of Christ's saving mission on earth and of St. Peter's essential role in the foundation of the Church.

St. Peter's Basilica, therefore, is not a museum, nor is it merely an extraordinary architectural achievement. It is a monument to faith. A monument that still in the 21st century proclaims to contemporary secular men and women that the greatest human endeavor is the effort to know God and His will and to embrace the salvation he has given to us through Jesus Christ. It is a salvation transmitted by his Church, of which St. Peter and his successor are Christ's vicars.

We can all be grateful to Fr. Jeffrey Kirby, whose knowledge and love of St. Peter's Basilica has produced this handsome volume. May its readers come to share his vibrant faith and his appreciation of this singular church.

*Rev. Msgr. Francis D. Kelly*
Canon of St. Peter's Basilica
Vatican City State

# 1

# The pope is the sovereign of his own country

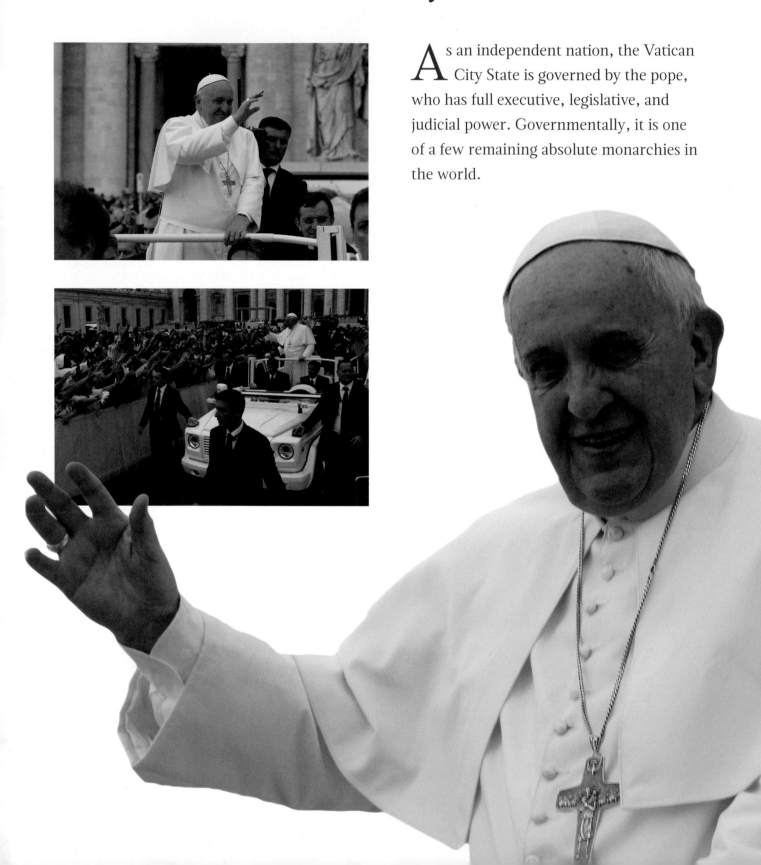

As an independent nation, the Vatican City State is governed by the pope, who has full executive, legislative, and judicial power. Governmentally, it is one of a few remaining absolute monarchies in the world.

# The Vatican's sovereignty has been recognized since the fourth century

The Church, under the term "Holy See," has been a recognized international government since the fourth century. The term refers to the pope's *sedes*, or chair, and is a symbol of the authority given to the pope by the Lord Jesus. The term "Holy See" distinctively refers to the Catholic Church as an international body, but also includes its temporal jurisdiction of the Vatican City State. As a recognized international body, the Holy See exchanges diplomatic relations with more than 180 countries, including the United States of America.

> "PRAISE the LORD, ALL NATIONS!"
>
> PSALM 117:1

# 3 The Vatican is the smallest country in the world

At 109 acres, about eight Vatican City States could fit within Central Park in New York City. While the Vatican is small, its independence assures the pope's freedom to teach and shepherd without coercion, interference, or hindrance from any other country or influence.

# The pope delegates some of his temporal powers

# 4

Legislative authority is given to the unicameral Pontifical Commission for Vatican City State, a group of Cardinals appointed by the pope for a five-year term. Executive authority is given to the President of this Commission, who has the title "President of the Governorate of Vatican City." Judicial authority is given to a Supreme Court consisting of three Cardinals. The judiciary also consists of several smaller courts, whose judges consist of both clergy and laity. In 2012, the butler of Pope Benedict XVI was tried by the Vatican Courts for leaking confidential information. In a televised five-day trial, he was found guilty and given an eighteen-month jail sentence, later suspended by the pope.

"FOR AS IN ONE BODY WE HAVE MANY MEMBERS, AND ALL THE MEMBERS DO NOT HAVE THE SAME FUNCTION."

—ROMANS 12:4

# 5
## The flag of the Vatican is square

The Vatican flag is one of two square country flags in the world (the other being Switzerland). Modeled on the infantry flag of the former Papal States, the Vatican flag consists of two vertical bands: one gold (hoist side) and the other white. The Vatican City State's coat-of-arms is placed on the white half of the flag. The coat-of-arms consists of the papal tiara (triple crown) with a gold key and a silver key crossed and held together by a red cord. In 1969, the Vatican flag was taken to the moon on the Apollo 11 mission. It was later returned to the pope, and can now be seen in the Vatican Museums.

# 6
## Latin is the official language of the Holy See

Although the operating language is predominately Italian, the Vatican City State uses Latin as its official language. As a consequence, Latin can be found throughout the Vatican, in government documents, on monuments, and stamps. Even the greeting on the automative teller machine, called a Bankomat, for the Vatican Bank is in Latin: *Insertio scidulam quaeso ut faciundam cognoscas rationem* (Insert your card for the account to be recognized).

# 7 The official office and residence of the pope is the Apostolic Palace

**W**hile many may hear the word "palace" and assume something grandiose, the word *palazzo*—translated as "palace"—can also mean simply "a large building." In seeing the Apostolic Palace, one understands that the residence is nothing like Buckingham Palace of London, but is really a simple collection of regular buildings that compose the pope's official residence and office.

# Pope Francis lives in the Domus Sanctae Marthae

# 8

Upon his election in 2013, Pope Francis surprised many people by deciding not to live in the official papal residence. The domus is actually a guesthouse—a hotel—in the back part of Vatican City. It was completed in 1996 as a residence for clergy and guests to the Vatican, as well as the official residence of the Cardinals when they are in Conclave to elect a new pope. Every morning of a Conclave, the Cardinals walk from the domus to the Sistine Chapel for discussion and voting.

# The pope is defended by the Pontifical Swiss Guard

Since the fifteenth century the popes have been defended by the Swiss Guard. Although they mostly perform ceremonial functions, the Guards are skilled soldiers in the Swiss Army, highly trained in security operations, who are sent to the Vatican and are committed to the pope's protection. There are approximately 130 men in the military unit. Their motto is "Fiercely and Faithfully" and refers to their defense of the pope. In commemoration of the heroic defense of the pope by the Swiss Guard during the Sack of Rome on May 6, 1527, the new members of the Guard take their solemn promise to the pope every May 6.

"I SWEAR *I will faithfully, loyally and honorably serve the Supreme Pontiff and his legitimate successors, and also dedicate myself to them with all my strength, sacrificing if necessary also my life to defend them. I assume this same commitment with regard to the Sacred College of Cardinals whenever the See is vacant.*

*Furthermore I promise to the Commanding Captain and my other superiors, respect, fidelity and obedience. This I swear! May God and our Holy Patrons assist me!*"

# The Vatican has a full range of public services

The Vatican has an active postal system with its own international country code: "SCV," just as the United States is "USA" and Italy is "IT." It holds only one zip code: 00120. It publishes its own stamps, most of which commemorate the Holy Father, his travels, or certain feast days and church anniversaries. The Vatican has its own criminal detention cells and police force, the Gendarmerie Corps, who are responsible for security, public order, criminal investigation, and other general police duties. The Vatican has its own bank, television center, newspaper, radio station, and internet registration—.va—as well as its own heliport, railway, grocery store, and pharmacy.

# 11 The Vatican has its own pre-seminary

The St. Pius X Pre-Seminary is a live-in school for boys ages 11–18. The pre-seminarians are known for their service as the altar boys of St. Peter's Basilica. Dressed in magenta cassocks, and appearing to be "little monsignors," the altar boys serve the array of morning Masses held every day on the multiple altars throughout the basilica. Every year, several of the pre-seminarians go on to enter college seminary and discern the priesthood.

# The Vatican's official currency is the Vatican euro

The most recent series of the Vatican euro was issued in March of 2014. The common side, which is used on every euro coin for all nations using the currency, is a map of Europe with twelve stars. On the other side, which nations are allowed to customize, the Vatican euro was diversified and three different coins were issued, each featuring a different image of the Pope Francis. The Vatican euro is highly-prized by collectors, leaving the Italian euro to serve as the operating currency of the Vatican.

# 13 The Vatican has no airplane for the pope's use

The Vatican City State has no airport and uses the public airports of Rome for the pope's travels. The Vatican will often use a borrowed Italian airliner or one from the host nation that the pope is visiting. The airplane is usually of normal design with no special features. Any plane that carries the pope, however, is given the name Shepherd One.

# The license plate of any vehicle carrying the pope is "SCV 1"

Of the different official cars used by the pope, the most famous is the popemobile. This is a specially engineered vehicle for outdoor public audiences that allows the pope to be visible to large crowds. There are different models of the popemobile that are used according to the occasion and anticipated security needs. Some popemobiles have a seat for the pope to rest in, and others can be sealed with bulletproof glass. All carry the license plate SVC 1. SCV stands for *Status Civitatis Vaticanae*, or "Vatican City State" in Latin.

# Succession of Popes

| | | | | | | |
|---|---|---|---|---|---|---|
| 1. St. Peter | 55. Boniface II | 109. St. Adrian III | 163. Honorius II | 217. Leo X |
| 2. St. Linus | 56. John II | 110. Stephen V | 164. Innocent II | 218. Adrian VI |
| 3. St. Anacletus | 57. St. Agapetus I | 111. Formosus | 165. Celestine II | 219. Clement VII |
| 4. St. Clement I | 58. St. Silverius | 112. Boniface VI | 166. Lucius II | 220. Paul III |
| 5. St. Evaristus | 59. Vigilius | 113. Stephen VI | 167. Bd. Eugene III | 221. Julius III |
| 6. St. Alexander I | 60. Pelagius I | 114. Romanus | 168. Anastasius IV | 222. Marcellus II |
| 7. St. Sixtus I | 61. John III | 115. Theodore II | 169. Adrian IV | 223. Paul IV |
| 8. St. Telesphorus | 62. Benedict I | 116. John IX | 170. Alexander III | 224. Pius IV |
| 9. St. Hyginus | 63. Pelagius II | 117. Benedict IV | 171. Lucius III | 225. St. Pius V |
| 10. St. Pius I | 64. St. Gregory I | 118. Leo V | 172. Urban III | 226. Gregory XIII |
| 11. St. Anicetus | 65. Sabinian | 119. Sergius III | 173. Gregory VIII, | 227. Sixtus V |
| 12. St. Soter | 66. Boniface III | 120. Anastasius III | 174. Clement III | 228. Urban VII |
| 13. St. Eleuterus | 67. St. Boniface IV | 121. Lando | 175. Celestine III | 229. Gregory XIV |
| 14. St. Victor I | 68. St. Deusdedit | 122. John X | 176. Innocent III | 230. Innocent IX |
| 15. St. Zephyrinus | 69. Boniface V | 123. Leo VI | 177. Honorius III | 231. Clement VIII |
| 16. St. Callixtus I | 70. Honorius I | 124. Stephen VII | 178. Gregory IX | 232. Leo XI |
| 17. St. Urban I | 71. Severinus | 125. John XI | 179. Celestine IV | 233. Paul V |
| 18. St. Pontian | 72. John IV | 126. Leo VII | 180. Innocent IV | 234. Gregory XV |
| 19. St. Anterus | 73. Theodore I | 127. Stephen VIII | 181. Alexander IV | 235. Urban VIII |
| 20. St. Fabian | 74. St. Martin I | 128. Marinus II | 182. Urban IV | 236. Innocent X |
| 21. St. Cornelius | 75. St. Eugene I | 129. Agapetus II | 183. Clement IV | 237. Alexander VII |
| 22. St. Lucius I | 76. St. Vitalian | 130. John XII | 184. Bd. Gregory X | 238. Clement IX |
| 23. St. Stephen I | 77. Adeodatus | 131. Benedict V | 185. Bd. Innocent V | 239. Clement X |
| 24. St. Sixtus II | 78. Donus | 132. Leo VIII | 186. Adrian V | 240. Bd. Innocent XI |
| 25. St. Dionysius | 79. St. Agatho | 133. John XIII | 187. John XXI | 241. Alexander VIII |
| 26. St. Felix I | 80. St. Leo II | 134. Benedict VI | 188. Nicholas III | 242. Innocent XII |
| 27. St. Eutychian | 81. St. Benedict II | 135. Benedict VII | 189. Martin IV | 243. Clement XI |
| 28. St. Caius | 82. John V | 136. John XIV | 190. Honorius IV | 244. Innocent XIII |
| 29. St. Marcellinus | 83. Conon | 137. John XV | 191. Nicholas IV | 245. Benedict XIII |
| 30. St. Marcellus I | 84. St. Sergius I | 138. Gregory V | 192. St. Celestine V | 246. Clement XII |
| 31. St. Eusebius | 85. John VI | 139. Sylvester II | 193. Boniface VIII | 247. Benedict XIV |
| 32. St. Miltiades | 86. John VII | 140. John XVII | 194. Bd. Benedict XI | 248. Clement XIII |
| 33. St. Sylvester I | 87. Sisinnius | 141. John XVIII | 195. Clement V | 249. Clement XIV |
| 34. St. Mark | 88. Constantine | 142. Sergius IV | 196. John XXII | 250. Pius VI |
| 35. St. Julius I | 89. St. Gregory II | 143. Benedict VIII | 197. Benedict XII | 251. Pius VII |
| 36. Liberius | 90. Gregory III | 144. John XIX | 198. Clement VI | 252. Leo XII |
| 37. St. Damasus I | 91. St. Zachary | 145. Benedict IX | 199. Innocent VI | 253. Pius VIII |
| 38. St. Siricius | 92. Stephen II | 146. Sylvester III | 200. Bd. Urban V | 254. Gregory XVI |
| 39. St. Anastasius I | 93. St. Paul I | 147. Benedict IX | 201. Gregory XI | 255. Bd. Pius IX |
| 40. St. Innocent I | 94. Stephen III | 148. Gregory VI | 202. Urban VI | 256. Leo XIII |
| 41. St. Zosimus | 95. Adrian I | 149. Clement II | 203. Boniface IX | 257. St. Pius X |
| 42. St. Boniface I | 96. St. Leo III | 150. Benedict IX | 204. Innocent VII | 258. Benedict XV |
| 43. St. Celestine I | 97. Stephen IV | 151. Damasus II | 205. Gregory XIII | 259. Pius XI |
| 44. St. Sixtus III | 98. St. Paschal I | 152. St. Leo IX | 206. Martin V | 260. Ven. Pius XII |
| 45. St. Leo I | 99. Eugene II | 153. Victor II | 207. Eugene IV | 261. St. John XXIII |
| 46. St. Hilarius | 100. Valentine | 154. Stephen IX | 208. Nicholas V | 262. Bd. Paul VI |
| 47. St. Simplicius | 101. Gregory IV | 155. Nicholas II | 209. Callixtus III | 263. John Paul I |
| 48. St. Felix III | 102. Sergius II | 156. Alexander II | 210. Pius II | 264. St. John Paul II |
| 49. St. Gelasius I | 103. St. Leo IV | 157. St. Gregory VII | 211. Paul II | 265. Benedict XVI |
| 50. Anastasius II | 104. Benedict III | 158. Bd. Victor III | 212. Sixtus IV | 266. Francis I |
| 51. St. Symmachus | 105. St. Nicholas I | 159. Bd. Urban II | 213. Innocent VIII | |
| 52. St. Hormisdas | 106. Adrian II | 160. Paschal II | 214. Alexander VI | |
| 53. St. John I | 107. John VIII | 161. Gelasius II | 215. Pius III | |
| 54. St. Felix IV | 108. Marinus I | 162. Callixtus II | 216. Julius II | |

# St. Peter was the first pope

**P**eter was appointed head of the Church by the Lord Jesus (cf. Matthew 16:16–18), and re-named (from Simon) by the Lord for this mission (cf. John 1:42). Since St. Peter, there have been 266 popes in an "unbroken chain."

## "HIS OFFICE LET ANOTHER TAKE."

—ACTS 1:20

# 16
## St. Peter was martyred in what is now Vatican City

St. Peter's martyrdom occurred in the Circus of Caligula-Nero on the Vatican Hill around the year 67 AD. St. Peter was sentenced to be crucified, but he asked and was granted permission by the Emperor Nero to be crucified upside down because he did not consider himself worthy to die in the same manner as the Lord Jesus.

### "I HAVE BEEN CRUCIFIED WITH CHRIST."

—GALATIANS 2:20

# 17
## Jesus prophesied St. Peter's martyrdom

St. John recounts in his Gospel that the Lord prophesied St. Peter's martyrdom, saying to him: "Truly, truly, I say to you, when you were young, you girded yourself and walked where you would; but when you are old, you will stretch out your hands, and another will gird you and carry you where you do not wish to go. (This he said to show by what death he [Peter] was to glorify God)" (John 21:18–19).

"GREATER LOVE HAS NO MAN THAN THIS, THAT A MAN LAY DOWN HIS LIFE FOR HIS FRIENDS."

—JOHN 15:13

# 18

## The body of St. Peter was retrieved by the early Christians

After his martyrdom, St. Peter was buried in the preexisting Necropolis (city of the dead) in the Imperial Gardens of the Vatican Hill. The burial site was disguised, and its location was secretly shared among the Christians of Rome. In large part, the bones have rested there since 67 AD, and the current basilica rests over this sacred place.

*"Thus says the Lord God to these bones: Behold, I will cause breath to enter you, and you shall live."* —EZEKIEL 37:5

# 19

## In securing St. Peter's body, the Christians were not able to recover his feet

The majority of St. Peter's body is accounted for by the Church, except the Apostle's feet. The early Christians had to act quickly in taking his body from the Circus of Caligula-Nero, and since the first pope had been crucified upside down, when they removed his body they could not take his feet.

# St. Peter's Basilica is not the pope's cathedral

St. Peter's Basilica is the esteemed sanctuary and resting place of the Apostle Peter making the Vatican the seat of government for the Church. But the actual cathedral of the pope as the Bishop of Rome is the Archbasilica of Christ the Savior. The archbasilica is commonly known as St. John Lateran, since it is dedicated to both St. John the Baptist and St. John the Evangelist, and is located in the historic neighborhood of the Lateran family. St. John Lateran is the oldest legal Christian Church in the world, given to the pope by the Emperor after the legalization of the Church in the fourth century.

# 21

# Pope John Paul II was the first non-Italian pope since 1523 AD

Elected in 1978, Pope John Paul II of Krakow, Poland, was the first non-Italian pope since 1523 AD. Pope Francis, elected in 2013, was the first pope from Latin America.

# The current St. Peter's is the second basilica on Vatican Hill

The first basilica on the ground of the Vatican was built by the Emperor Constantine in the fourth century. Although highly controversial, Pope Julius II decided to build a new basilica because of the neglect to the first basilica while the popes lived in southern France (1309–1377 AD). The new basilica was begun in 1506 and took nearly 120 years, seven chief architects, and twenty popes to complete. It was built during the Renaissance and included the work of such artistic masters as Raphael, Michelangelo, Fontana, Della Porta, Maderno, and Bramante. On account of their involvement, St. Peter's Basilica is hailed as the crown of the Renaissance.

"HOW LOVELY IS THY DWELLING PLACE, O LORD OF HOSTS!"

—PSALM 84:1

# 23

# The World Series could be played in the space of St. Peter's Square

St. Peter's Square was designed after the construction and papal consecration of the new basilica. It was completed by the Baroque master, Bernini, between 1656–1667 AD. Today, the great Square greets pilgrim and visitor alike.

It is 1,000 feet long and 750 feet wide. Wrigley Field could fit within the square twice (with space to spare). The World Series could be played in St. Peter's Square, and approximately 250,000 people can fit within it.

# The Square is actually an oval formed by two semicircles of columns

Each semi-circle of Saint Peter's square consists of two double rows of columns which are 64 feet high each. The space between the rows is 16 feet—enough for two cars to drive side-by-side.

# 25 The semicircles of the colonnades represent the maternal arms of the Church

*"O Jerusalem, Jerusalem, killing the prophets and stoning those who are sent to you! How often would I have gathered your children together as a hen gathers her brood under her wings, and you would not!"*

—MATTHEW 23:37

# 140 great saints line the tops of the colonnades of St. Peter's Square

The statues on the top of the colonnades of St. Peter's Square represent prominent saints and founders of different religious orders. Each statue is 10 feet high. Their presence reminds us of all the saints in heaven, the "cloud of witnesses" that is with every believer in the walk of discipleship (cf. Hebrews 12:1).

# 27 The oval shape represents the Providence of God over all things

The oval shape of St. Peter's Square represents the order of the cosmos. The obelisk holds center place and serves as a symbol of the sun and a sundial in the square. Radiating lines of white travertine span from the obelisk and run throughout the square representing the universe. Circular stones are set to indicate the location of the sun's shadow as it enters each of the signs of the zodiac. This wonderful display shows a type of map of the universe and the sanctifying of time and seasons by the grace of God.

*"For it is he who gave me unerring knowledge of what exists, to know the structure of the world and the activity of the elements; the beginning and end and middle of times, the alternations of the solstices and then changes of the seasons, the cycles of the year and the constellations of the stars, . . . for wisdom, the fashioner of all things taught me."*

—WISDOM 17:17–19, 22

# In the center of the square is an obelisk from Egypt

The obelisk is a single red granite stone, standing 135 feet high and weighing approximately 312 tons. In Egyptian mythology, the obelisk was intended to represent the umbilical cord between the gods and humanity. Placed in St. Peter's Square and topped with a Cross, the symbolism is perfected. The obelisk now represents the center of the cosmos and the full union between God and humanity in Jesus Christ, and the union of Christ with His Church.

"FOR THERE IS ONE GOD, AND THERE IS ONE MEDIATOR, BETWEEN GOD AND MEN, THE MAN CHRIST JESUS, WHO GAVE HIMSELF AS A RANSOM FOR ALL."

—1 TIMOTHY 2:5–6

# St. Peter's Square

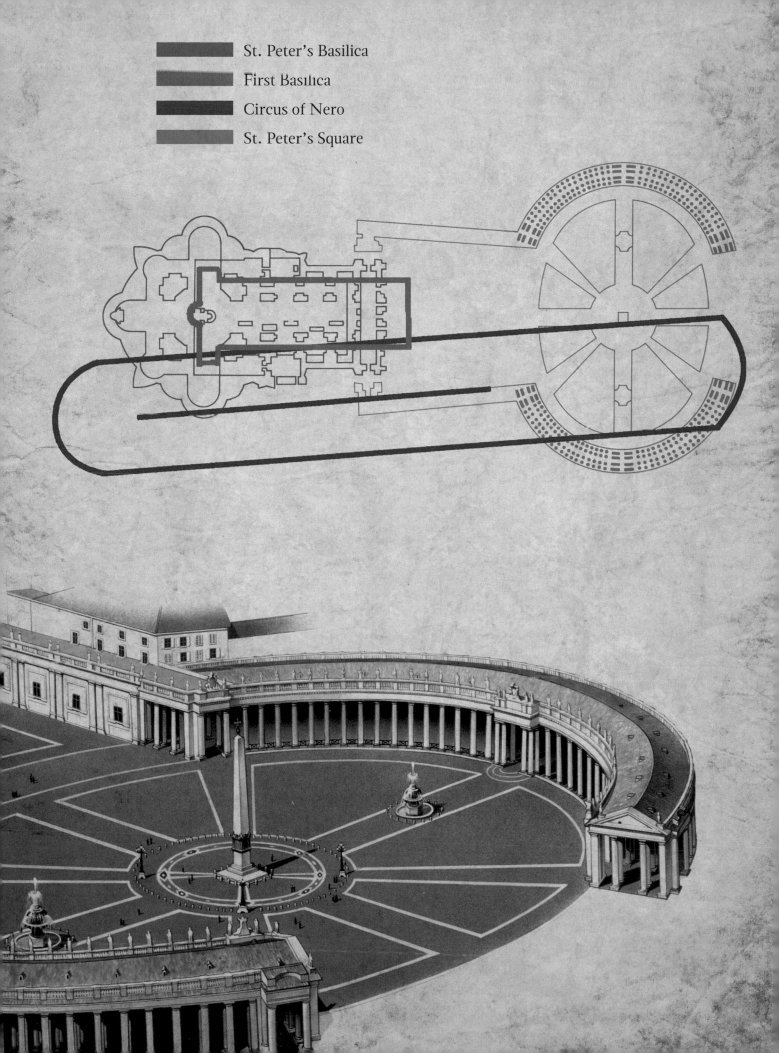

St. Peter's Basilica

First Basilica

Circus of Nero

St. Peter's Square

# 29

## The obelisk was moved to its current location in 1586 AD

During the time of the Emperor Nero, the obelisk was in the center of the Circus of Caligula-Nero. In ancient Rome, a "circus" was a large open space for public events, similar to a contemporary racetrack. In 67 AD, when St. Peter was brought to the circus, he was crucified in plain view of the obelisk. It was one of the last things the blessed Apostle saw, and so Christian tradition considers the obelisk a kind of visual relic of St. Peter. It was moved to its current location in 1586—this was an extraordinary four-month undertaking that involved 900 workers, 140 horses, and 47 winches.

# 30

## The obelisk extols Christ as conqueror

On the side of the obelisk facing the outside of the square, a Latin inscription reads:

ECCE CRUX DOMINI FUGITE
PARTES ADVERSAE
VICIT LEO DE TRIBU IUDA

"Behold, the Cross of the Lord, fly you enemies; The Lion of the Tribe of Judah has conquered."

On the side of the obelisk facing the basilica, another Latin inscription reads:

CHRISTUS VINCIT CHRISTUS
REGNAT CHRISTUS IMPERAT
CHRISTUS AB OMNI MALO
PLEBEM SUAM DEFENDAT

"Christ conquers, Christ reigns, Christ rules; May Christ guard his people against all evil."

# 31

# There is a marker where Pope St. John Paul II was shot

On the right side of St. Peter's Square, facing the basilica, a small marker is on the ground. It is a simple gray stone, with the coat of arms of Pope St. John Paul II, and the date May 13, 1981 in Roman numerals. It commemorates the place and the date of the attempted assassination of John Paul II.

During his regular Wednesday audience, while moving through the crowds, the pope was shot and severely wounded. The wounds from the gunshot should have taken his life, but for no medical reason, the bullet moved within the pope's body and his life was spared.

# There was no image of the Blessed Virgin Mary in St. Peter's Square until 1981

# 32

When the unexplained movement of the bullet from the attempted assassination was told to Pope John Paul II, he said: "One hand shot (the would-be assassin) and another hand guided (the Blessed Virgin Mary)." The assassination attempt had been made on May 13, the feast of Our Lady of Fatima, and John Paul II credited Our Lady of Fatima with saving his life. In honor of Mary's intervention, the pope placed the would-be assassin's bullet in the crown of Our Lady while on a pilgrimage to Fatima in 1982. The pope also ordered a mosaic image of Mary to be placed overlooking St. Peter's Square. Surprisingly, this was the first image of Mary to adorn the square. No other image or statue of Mary was present until the mosaic was placed there in December of 1981.

# 33

## A Latin dedication spans the façade of St. Peter's Basilica

At 377 feet long and 148 feet high, the front of the basilica welcomes all people. An inscription in Latin is immediately visible. Translated, it reads:

"In honor of the Prince of the Apostles; Paul V Borghese, Supreme Pontiff, in the year 1612, the seventh of his pontificate."

# Statues of St. Peter and St. Paul stand on either side of the façade

St. Peter and St. Paul serve as patrons of the city of Rome. As ancient Rome was founded by the mythical Romulus and Remus, Christian Rome is founded on the blood of these two glorious martyrs. Peter is seen holding the keys of the kingdom (cf. Matthew 16:19) and a tablet, since two letters of the New Testament are attributed to him. Paul is seen with a sword, since the word of God is active, sharper than any two-edged sword (cf. Hebrews 4:12). It also symbolizes St. Paul's martyrdom by the sword. He, too, is shown with a tablet since several letters in the New Testament are attributed to his authorship.

*"For the word of God is living and active, sharper than any two-edged sword, piercing to the division of soul and spirit, of joints and marrow, and discerning the thoughts and intentions of the heart."*
—HEBREWS 4:12

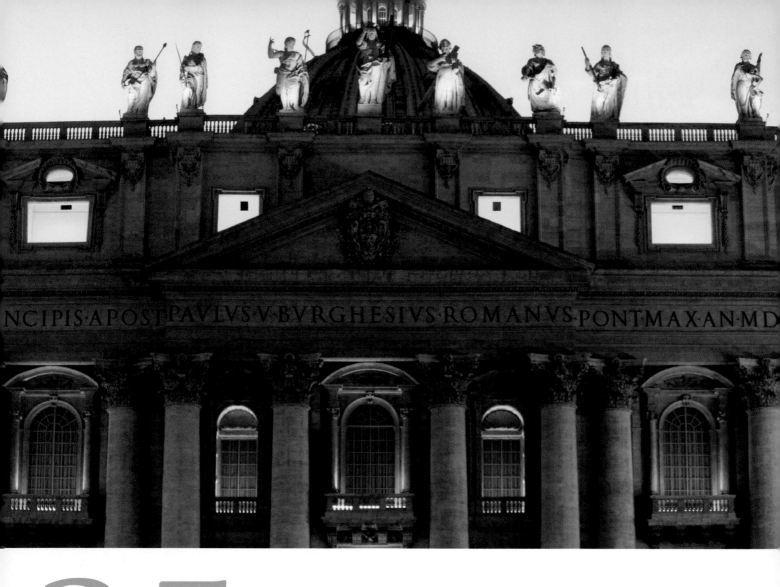

NCIPIS·APOST·PAVLVS·V·BVRGHESIVS·ROMANVS·PONT·MAX·AN·MD

# 35 From the center of the façade each new pope is announced to the world

On a small balcony in the center of the façade known as the Loggia of Benedictions, each new pope is announced to the world. From this spot the new pope makes his first appearance and gives his papal blessing. The central balcony is also used by the pope on Christmas and Easter to give the *Urbi et Orbi* blessing addressed to the city and to the world. During this blessing, the pope prays for specific concerns of humanity and asks for God's favor. Beneath the balcony is a marble bas-relief sculpture of Jesus giving the keys of the kingdom to St. Peter.

# St. Peter's Basilica

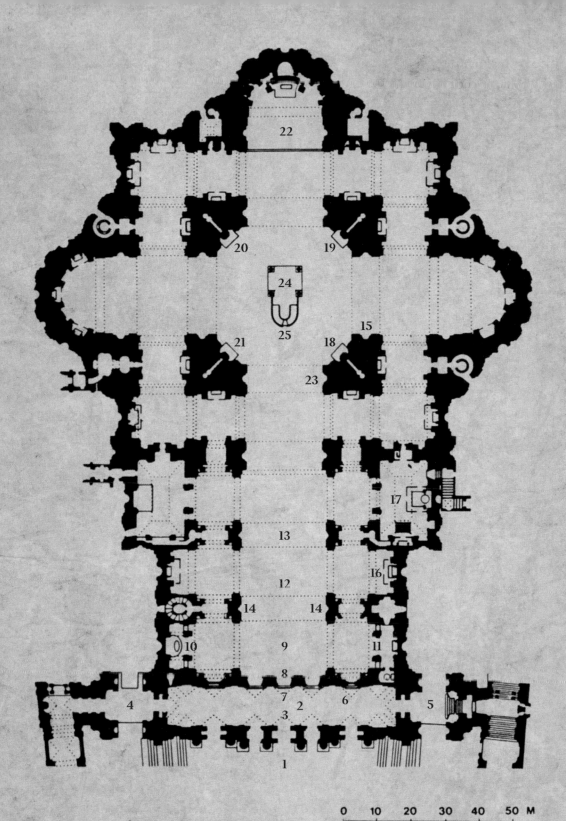

| | | |
|---|---|---|
| **1.** St. Peter's Square | **10.** Baptistry and Baptismal Font (#45) | **18.** Statue of Longinus (#62) |
| **2.** Portico (#37) | **11.** Pieta Statue (#48) | **19.** Statue of Queen Helena (#63) |
| **3.** Navicella Mosaic | **12.** Nave (#52) | **20.** Statue of Veronica (#64) |
| **4.** Statue of Charlemagne | **13.** Brass Church Markers (#53) | **21.** Statue of St. Andrew (#66) |
| **5.** Statue of Constantine | **14.** Holy Water Fonts x2 (#55) | **22.** Chapel of the Chair (#70) |
| **6.** Holy Doors (#41) | **15.** Statue of Mother Cabrini | **23.** Bronze Statue of St. Peter (#76) |
| **7.** Filarete Doors (#42) | **16.** Altar of St. Sebastian—Burial Place | **24.** Altar of Confession (#78) |
| **8.** Templum Vaticanum Marker (#43) | of Pope St. John Paul II (#58) | **25.** Ninety-Nine Vigil Candles (#100) |
| **9.** Royal Porphyry Circle (#44) | **17.** Adoration Chapel (#59) | |

# 36 Visitors to St. Peter's must pass by "the modesty police"

Visitors to St. Peter's pass first through a metal detector, and then through an usher station, jokingly called "the modesty police." The basilica has a strict dress code to ensure modesty. For both men and women, clothing must reach the knees and shoulders must be covered. If anyone wishes to pray, they can go to any of the over 900 churches in Rome. But if they choose to pray at St. Peter's Basilica, they must follow the clothing requirements posted throughout the security area.

# Statues of two emperors flank the portico to St. Peter's Basilica

## 37

On the far left of the portico to St. Peter's is a statue of Charlemagne, and on the far right is a statue of Constantine. Both statues recall earlier centuries and honor these emperors who were patrons of the basilica and the Church. Immortalized in stone, they stand as perpetual protectors of the church building and of the living Church that inspired it.

# 38 Massive bells sound the death—and election—of each pope

The Arch of the Bells in St. Peter's houses the massive bells used to sound the death toll for each pope and rouse the faithful to mourn. A new practice, begun by the Conclave of 2005, is the announcement of a new pope by both the white smoke of the Sistine Chapel and the ringing of the bells in the Arch of the Bells.

# The *Navicella* mosaic reminds us of the Lord's saving presence

The *Navicella* (little ship) mosaic is above the entrance to the portico. It was made by the Umbrian artist, Giotto, for the first Jubilee Year in 1300 AD, and is one of the few works of art that was also in the first basilica. The mosaic shows St. Peter sinking in the waters of the Sea of Galilee and being rescued by the Lord Jesus (cf. Matthew 14:28–33). Giotto was so inspired by the Gospel story that he placed himself in the work. In the lower, left-hand corner, we see Giotto fishing on the shore and watching the scene.

"LORD, SAVE ME!"
—MATTHEW 14:30

# 40

## The portico features various biblical scenes from St. Peter's life

Scenes from the life of St. Peter, such as the healing of his mother-in-law and walking on water, are located on the central panels of the vaults of the basilica's portico. These recall the humanity of the Apostle and remind visitors and pilgrims of actual accounts in the saint's life. Along the edge of the portico, there are statues of the first thirty-one successors of St. Peter, all of whom are revered as martyrs for the Faith. Before the legal toleration of Christianity beginning in 313 AD, it was considered a death sentence to be elected pope.

# 41

## The Holy Doors are only opened once every twenty-five years

The Holy Doors of St. Peter's are only opened by the pope for Jubilee Years, which are ordinarily held every twenty-five years. The Jubilee Year is a devotional revival of the Old Testament practice, and is announced as an appointed time of grace and conversion, hope and joy. The last Jubilee Year was in the year 2000. Panels on the Holy Doors depict the damnation and salvation of humanity, the ministry of the Lord Jesus to sinners, and the Resurrection.

"AND I TELL YOU, ASK, AND IT WILL BE GIVEN TO YOU; SEEK, AND YOU WILL FIND; KNOCK, AND IT WILL BE OPENED TO YOU."

—LUKE 11:9

# 42 Despite their size, a small child could open the massive Filarete Doors

Called the Filarete Doors, after the Florentine master who designed them, the central doors of St. Peter's show Christ as Savior of the World and Mary as Full of Grace. St. Peter and St. Paul are also represented, and beneath their images are panels that depict their respective martyrdoms: Peter by crucifixion upside down, and Paul beheaded by the sword. Although massive in size, the doors are opened and closed through a controlled system of springs and weights. A small child could easily open the great Filarete Doors without effort.

# St. Peter's takes up nearly ten acres

Just beyond the Filarete Doors, the *Templum Vaticanum* brass identifier marks St. Peter's Basilica as the largest Christian church in the world. The basilica is 432,756 square feet (including the side-chapels and sacristy). From the left transept (wing of the church) to the right transept, the basilica measures 461 feet in width. At 694 feet, the length of the basilica (including the portico) is almost as long as two American football fields. The Super Bowl could be played in the nave, the center aisle, of the basilica. Besides the great dome, the basilica has ten other domes over side chapels. In all, the basilica has 290 windows, 597 pillars, 44 altars, and approximately 135 mosaics and 435 statues. Within its body, the basilica could accommodate 100,000 people (although papal liturgies are usually limited to around 60,000).

# 44 A purple circle marks the spot where Charlemagne was crowned Emperor

At the entrance of the nave, there is a large porphyry circle. "Porphyry" comes from a Latin word meaning "purple," and is a rare igneous rock. The porphyry circle was preserved from the first basilica. Emperors and kings knelt upon it to kiss the Cross and to recite the Creed before they went to the tomb of the Apostle Peter to be anointed and crowned. Most prominently, Charlemagne was crowned Holy Roman Emperor on this purple circle by Pope Leo III in 800 AD. In the old basilica, the circle was in the sanctuary. In the new basilica, it was placed at the entrance to signify that all those who enter the Church through baptism enter a royal priesthood.

*"Come to him, to that living stone, rejected by men but in God's sight chosen and precious; and like living stones be yourselves built into a spiritual house, to be a holy priesthood, to offer spiritual sacrifices acceptable to God through Jesus Christ."*

—1 PETER 2:4–5

# The baptistry is the birthplace of the royal priesthood of all believers

The baptismal font, or baptistry, is heralded by a large, gilded image of a Lamb. On the forepart of the font, two angels hold a relief of the Holy Trinity. The font consists of a large reddish porphyry basin. At 12 feet long and 6 feet broad, the basin is said to have been a part of Emperor Hadrian's tomb. Now, it is the source of eternal life through baptism.

*"Do you not know that all of us who have been baptized into Christ Jesus were baptized into his death? We were buried therefore with him by baptism into death, so that as Christ was raised from the dead by the glory of the Father, we too might walk into newness of life."*

—ROMANS 6:3–4

# 46 Images of baptisms from the Bible adorn the baptistry

The baptistry of St. Peter's is covered with beautiful mosaics. The central image is of Jesus Christ being baptized in the Jordan River by St. John the Baptist. The side mosaics, however, could be easily missed but are very important as they emphasize St. Peter's role in the decision to welcome Gentiles into the early Church (cf. Acts 15:7–11). The mosaics show St. Peter baptizing his converted guards, Saints Processus and Martinianus, in the Mamertine Prison, as well as St. Peter baptizing the Gentile centurion Cornelius.

# Allegorical images depicting the three forms of baptism adorn the dome

# 47

The mosaic images in the dome of the baptistry are of the baptism in the Jordan, a depiction of martyrdom, and a scene of hordes of people eagerly awaiting baptism. These are meant as an allegory of the triple baptismal forms of water, blood, and desire.

"AND MARY SAID, 'MY SOUL MAGNIFIES THE LORD,
AND MY SPIRIT REJOICES IN GOD MY SAVIOR.'"

—LUKE 1:46

# To the right of the entrance is the *Pieta*— the world's most famous religious sculpture

The *Pieta* (which means "pity" in Italian), is also known as *The Deposition*. It is perhaps the world's most famous religious sculpture. It depicts the Blessed Virgin Mary holding her deceased Son after His torturous Passion and Death. As the statue stands at the entrance of the basilica, so Mary stands as a guide and help to all disciples of the Lord Jesus. Never a barrier, but always a bridge, Mary seeks to help all people to draw closer to her divine Son.

"AND MARY SAID, 'BEHOLD, I AM THE HANDMAID OF THE LORD; LET IT BE TO ME ACCORDING TO YOUR WORD.'"

—LUKE 1:38

# The *Pieta* was carved from a single block of white Carrara marble

The *Pieta*, at 6 feet wide and 5 feet, 9 inches high, was made by Michelangelo from a single block of white Carrara marble between 1498–1500 AD. It was commissioned by the French envoy to the pope for St. Petronilla's chapel in the old basilica, and was unveiled for the Jubilee Year of 1500.

# 50

## The *Pieta* is the only autographed work of Michelangelo

After the *Pieta's* unveiling Michelangelo overheard people attributing the work to other artists and became enraged. He placed the inscription, "Michelangelo Buonarroti, Florentine, Maker" on a small ribbon across the statue's chest. Later, however, he returned and was filled with remorse over this display of pride. To counter his vanity, the artist made a private vow never to sign another work of art, and he remained faithful to that vow. The *Pieta* is the only autographed work of Michelangelo.

# 51

## The *Pieta* depicts Mary as a young woman

Despite the fact that Mary was 45–50 years old at the time of the Lord's death, some speculate that Michelangelo, who lost his mother when he was five years old, used childhood memories of his mother's own face as a model for Mary's face. The youthful portrayal, however, can also be supported by Mary's special status as one free from sin and full of grace.

## "BEHOLD, YOUR MOTHER!"

—JOHN 19:27

# The Super Bowl could be played in the 611-foot nave

Nave comes from the Latin word meaning "ship." It was an addition by the master artist Maderno to Michelangelo's original design. The new plan required the elongation of the eastern wing to 611 feet, which is now the nave of the second St. Peter's Basilica.

"... THE HOUSEHOLD OF GOD, WHICH IS THE CHURCH OF THE LIVING GOD, THE PILLAR AND BULWARK OF THE TRUTH."

—1 TIMOTHY 3:15

# 53 Brass markers on the floor of the nave show the size of other churches

Markers in the nave of St. Peter's show the length of other famous churches throughout the world. Measuring from the Altar of the Chair to the end of the nave, each marker indicates how these other major churches compare in length and size to St. Peter's Basilica. The markers are not merely an exercise in trivia, but an expression of the universal nature of the Church. They are a reminder that no believer walks alone. Among the many markers, there are citations for churches in London (519 feet), Brussels (462 feet), Cologne (443 feet), Paris (427 feet), Seville (433 feet), Mexico City (392 feet), Istanbul (359 feet), Sydney (376 feet), and Brasilia (366 feet). From the United States, there are markers for Boston (358 feet), New York (332 feet), Washington, DC (457 feet), and most recently, Los Angeles (396 feet).

*"So then you are no longer strangers and sojourners, but you are fellow citizens with the saints and members of the household of God."*

—EPHESIANS 2:19

# Scripture verses proclaiming the pope's authority line the nave

54

Scripture verses on a field of gold line the edges of the nave. Each black letter is about 6 feet tall. An average-sized person, with raised arms, would fit completely within one "O" of the verses. On the left side of the nave, recounting the solemn words of Jesus to Peter, the Latin verse reads:

EGO ROGAVI PRO TE, O PETRE,
UT NON DEFICIAT FIDES TUA:
ET TU ALIQUANDO CONVERSES
CONFIRMA FRATERS TUOS

*"But I have prayed for you that your faith may not fail; and when you have turned again, strengthen your brethren" (Luke 22:32).*

On the right side of the nave, recalling the commission of Christ to Peter, the Latin verse reads:

QUODCUMQUE LIGAVERIS
SUPER TERRAM, ERIT
LIGATUM ETIN COELIS:
ET QUODCUMQUE SOLVERIS
SUPER TERRAM, ERIT SOLUTUM
ET IN COELI

*"And whatever you bind on earth shall be bound in heaven, and whatever you loose on earth shall be loosed in heaven"* (Matthew 16:19).

BASES · PILARVM

EX · LAPIDE · TIBVRTINO · MARMOREAE

IX PONTIFICATVS · AN · XIII

# 55

# Massive holy water fonts are found at the entrance to the nave

On both sides of the nave, a pair of angels present the holy water font to the faithful reminding us of our baptism. The masterful use of proportion can be seen as we consider that, if the angels were to step out and stand up, they would be about 6 feet tall. These angels, and the angels represented throughout the basilica, symbolize the unseen realities of the spiritual life and of the enduring presence of angels who guard and protect the faithful.

*"Do not neglect to show hospitality to strangers, for thereby some have entertained angels unawares."*

—HEBREWS 13:2

# Statues of saints adorn the pillars of the nave

The pillars of the nave have two statues, one on a lower niche and one above it. The statues below are about 16 feet tall, while the statues above are about 20 feet tall. The difference is proportioned so that the lower and upper statues would appear to be the same size from the nave. Among the thirty-nine saints represented are St. Vincent de Paul, St. Ignatius of Loyola, St. Alphonsus Liguori, St. Benedict, St. Angela Merici, and St. Frances Xavier Cabrini, who was the first American citizen to be canonized and is the only American represented in the entire basilica.

*"Therefore, since we are surrounded by so great a cloud of witnesses, let us also lay aside every weight, and sin which clings so closely, and let us run with perseverance the race that is set before us."*

—HEBREWS 12:1

# 57 In the nave 28 female sculptures represent the virtues

Along the perimeter of the nave, on the transepts and above the arches, twenty-eight Christian and human virtues are represented. Each is depicted as a female figure. The virtues are present because they assist us in seeking God, who is All-Good. They are symbolized as beautiful women in order to show us the attraction virtue has on the person of good will. Unlike the pomp and seduction of vice, the real beauty of virtue is free and sober-minded.

# The Altar of St. Sebastian is the resting place of Pope St. John Paul II

The altar to the right of the nave is dedicated to St. Sebastian, patron of athletes and soldiers. However, it is most well-known as the resting place of the body of Pope St. John Paul II. He was moved to this altar after his beatifica-tion. The tomb of the third longest-serv-ing pope in the history of the Catholic Church is highly revered and visited by thousands every week. Special ushers are assigned to facilitate the large crowds at the tomb throughout the day.

# The Adoration Chapel is a place of perpetual prayer

Talking, loud actions, or photographs are not permitted in the Adoration Chapel. Ushers are posted to enforce these expectations. The chapel is a place of prayer, a reminder that the entire basilica is a house of worship. St. Peter's is not a museum, a display in art appreciation, or a laboratory for architectural design. It is a place to give honor and praise to the living God.

*"One thing I have asked of the Lord, that will I seek after; that I may dwell in the house of the Lord all the days of my life, to behold the beauty of the Lord and to inquire in his temple."*

—PSALM 27:4

# 60 Massive columns are needed to support the weight of the dome

The four columns of the sanctuary each have a circumference of 233 feet, and are necessary to help hold the immense weight of the dome. On each of the spandrels, which is the space below the circular drum in-between the arches of the columns, there is a 28-foot mosaic medallion of one of the Evangelists, illustrating that they are the grand pillars of the Church. From their four Gospel books, we receive the gospel of Jesus Christ.

*"How beautiful upon the mountains are the feet of him who brings good tidings of good, who publishes salvation."*

—ISAIAH 52:7

# 61 On each column, an image depicts one of the Evangelists

Each of the columns of St. Peter's Basilica is associated with an Evangelist, with an image of an ox, a lion, an eagle, and a man representing respectively St. Matthew, St. Mark, St. Luke and St. John.

These creatures became associated with their respective Evangelists because the beginning of each Gospel seems to correspond to a living creature's appearance. For example, St. Mark begins his Gospel with St. John the Baptist crying in the wilderness like a lion (cf. Mark 1:2–3) and so St. Mark is depicted by a lion. The images convey that the Evangelists were guided by God in the writing of their Gospels, that the Gospels are the Word of God and a pillar of our faith.

# A statue of St. Longinus adorns the northeast column

Longinus was the Roman centurion who pierced the side of Jesus with a lance on the Cross. In the experience of Christ's death, he was converted to the Christian faith (cf. Mark 15:39). The statue is about 15 feet tall, and was made by Bernini from 1635–1638 AD. In 1492, fragments of Longinus' lance were given to Pope Innocent VIII by Sultan Bajazet, son of Mohomet II.

*"And when the centurion, who stood facing him, saw that he thus breathed his last, he said, 'Truly this man was the Son of God!'"*

—MARK 15:39

# 63 On the northwest column, St. Helena holds the Cross

Helena was the mother of Emperor Constantine, and is honored as having found the True Cross of Jesus Christ in Jerusalem. Her statue in St. Peter's is about 15 feet tall, and was carved by Andrea Bolgi from 1629–1639.

# The actual veil of Veronica is housed in the reliquary chapel above her statue

Veronica, the unknown woman who charitably wiped the face of Jesus during his Passion, stands atop the southwest pillar. In gratitude Jesus left his sacred countenance on the cloth. Not knowing her name, pious tradition has simply called her by the name of the gift she received: *vera icona* (true icon). Her statue is about 16 feet tall, and was sculpted by Francesco Mochi from 1629–1640. The actual veil of Veronica is housed in the reliquary chapel above the statue. The master poet Dante (1265–1321 AD) saw the veil during the Jubilee Year of 1300, and exalts it in the *Paradiso* of his *Divine Comedy*.

# The head of St. Andrew was once housed above his statue

## 65

St. Andrew was the younger brother of St. Peter and one of Jesus' first disciples. He is attached to an "X" cross symbolizing how he was martyred. His statue is 15 feet tall, and was sculpted by Francois Duquesnoy. It was unveiled in the presence of Pope Urban VIII in 1640.

The reliquary chapel once housed the head of St. Andrew; however, in 1966, Pope Paul VI gave the relic to the church of St. Andrew in Patras, Greece, as a sign of friendship with the Greek Orthodox Church.

# St. Andrew's statue shows the Apostle's unique ministry in the Gospels

## 66

Three of the four statues adorning the massive columns of the basilica represent figures that are associated in some way with the Passion of the Lord Jesus. Andrew's presence, therefore, could cause some confusion, until we remember his role in the Gospels. St. Peter met Jesus through St. Andrew, his younger brother (John 1:41), and when the Greeks wanted to talk with Jesus, they went through St. Andrew (John 12:22). The Apostle Andrew could be seen as a type of secretary of Jesus, a kind of passageway. St. Andrew continues that ministry in the basilica built to honor his brother. The chief passageway to the crypt of the basilica, where St. Peter and the popes of old are buried, is behind the statue of St. Andrew. His statue marks the way to enter the lower level of the church.

## "WE WISH TO SEE JESUS."

—JOHN 12:21

# 67 Original columns from the first basilica adorn the various chapels above the statues

They are decorated with vine leaves, and are crowned with a relief, which refers to the chapel's respective relic. The relics of the different statues—the True Cross, Veronica's Veil, and Longinus' Lance—however, are not in their original sites. These three relics relating to the Passion are now kept together in the chapel above Veronica's statue. They are solemnly displayed in the basilica every year on the Fifth Sunday of Lent.

# 68 There is a hidden message surrounding the Altar of the Confession

E ach of the four main columns has a Latin inscription. Starting from the northwest pillar and moving clockwise, they read:

Northwest:   MUNDO REFULGET
Northeast:   HINC SACERDOTII
Southeast:   UNITAS EXORITUR
Southwest:   HINC UNA FIDES

Placed together, the sentence is translated as: "From here shines out to the world the oneness of the priesthood; from here there arises one faith." The message draws attention to the royal priesthood of the baptized and to the sacramental work celebrated in the sanctuary of the basilica.

# Scripture verses about Peter adorn the Sanctuary

On the left transept of the sanctuary is an inscription in Latin, which reads:

DICIT TER TIBI, PETRE, IESUS: DILIGIS ME? AIT ILLI: ETIAM DOMINE, TU SCIS QUIA AMO TE.

*"He said to him the third time, 'Peter, do you love me?' And he said to him, 'Lord, you know that I love you'" (John 21:17).*

Along the right transept, the verse reads:

O PETERE, DIXISTI, TU ES CHRISTUS, FILIUS DEI VIVI. AIT IESUS: BEATUS ES, SIMON BAR IONA: QUIA CARO ET SANGUIS NON RELEVAVIT TIBI.

*"Peter said, 'You are the Christ, the Son of the living God.' And Jesus answered him, 'Blessed are you, Simon, son of Jonah: for flesh and blood has not revealed this to you'" (Matthew 16:16–17).*

# 70

## The *Chair of St. Peter* is a symbol of service

The large bronze *Chair of St. Peter* sits in the chapel behind the main altar and displays the three offices of the Church: to teach, to govern, and to sanctify. It is not meant to be a regal throne with an empty assertion of power, but rather an authentic reflection of the office entrusted by the Lord Jesus to St. Peter and his successors. As an office given by Christ, the chair is a symbol of responsibility and service.

*"You know that the rulers of the Gentiles lord it over them, and their great men exercise authority over them. It shall not be so among you; but whoever would be great among you must be your servant, and whoever would be first among you must be your slave."*

—MATTHEW 20:25–27

# 71

# The bronze chair contains
# St. Peter's original chair

Bernini's bronze chair encloses a wooden chair inlaid with ivory, which was once believed to have been the chair presented to St. Peter by the Senator Prudens and used by the Apostle while preaching in Rome. It is now known to be a chair given to the papacy by one of the ninth century emperors.

# St. Peter's Chair appears to float

Four Doctors of the Church flank the chair. At 18 feet tall, the figures depict St. John Chrysostom and St. Athanasius from the East, and St. Augustine and St. Ambrose from the West. They hold a loop that is attached to the legs of the great chair. Such an action gives the statue the appearance of floating. The statues symbolize how the Church relies on human knowledge. The doctors, however, are only holding loops. They are not themselves sustaining the chair because the Church's authority is sustained solely by the power of the Holy Spirit.

*"But the Counselor, the Holy Spirit, whom the Father will send in my name, he will teach you all things."*

—JOHN 14:26

# 73

# Bernini's Holy Spirit Window, "Gloria," is not actually stained glass

The basilica has no stained glass. The Gloria window is oftentimes confused as stained glass, but it is actually thinly-cut alabaster. The window, which sits over the *Chair of Peter*, portrays the image of a dove arrayed in light. The wingspan of the dove is 6 feet and it holds a central place in the Chapel of the Chair. The window itself is divided into twelve sections, to honor the Twelve Apostles. A large, gold-colored cloud, which encircles the chair emanates from the window.

*". . . The household of God, built upon the foundation of the apostles and prophets, Christ Jesus himself being the cornerstone."*

—EPHESIANS 2:19-20

# An inscription hails the "Shepherd of the Church" in Latin and Greek

74

A single inscription flanks the chair— in Latin on the left side, in Greek on the right, it reads:

O PASTOR ECCLESIAE, TU OMNES CHRISTI PASCIS AGNOS ET OVES

"O Shepherd of the Church, you feed all the lambs and sheep of Christ" (cf. John 21:15–17). Repeating the phrase in two languages shows the universality of the Church.

# 75 Artwork around the chapel extol martyrdom and poverty

The vault of the Chapel of the Chair contains three panels. The central panel shows the Lord Jesus giving the keys of the kingdom to St. Peter. The panel to the left depicts St. Peter's crucifixion, and the panel on the right illustrates the beheading of St. Paul. The statues in the Chapel of the Chair are the founders of the mendicant (begging) orders of the Church, including St. Francis of Assisi and St. Dominic Guzman—giving honor to the great exemplars of evangelical poverty.

# The feet of St. Peter's statue have been worn down

The figure of the chief Apostle sits nobly in the right transept of the basilica. The feet of the statue, especially its right foot, have been worn down by the pious caresses of pilgrims throughout the centuries. This is ironic since the statue is in close proximity to the resting place of St. Peter, which holds most of the saint's body, except his feet. The statue seems to share the fate of the actual Apostle.

# 77

# The statue depicts St. Peter wearing a sling

The sling demonstrates the humanity of St. Peter. It is a reminder of human weakness and is an important lesson on the weight of the keys of Christ's authority: It is too heavy to bear without God's help. The pope, and all who are shepherds in the Church, must rely not on themselves but on the power of the Holy Spirit.

*"But [Jesus] said to me, 'My grace is sufficient for you, for my power is made perfect in weakness.'"*

—2 CORINTHIANS 12:9

# The Altar of the Confession sits directly over St. Peter's bones

# 78

The altar is named for Peter's confession of faith: "You are the Christ, the Son of the living God." (Matthew 16:16). It is the third altar to sit over St. Peter's tomb: the first was built by Pope St. Gregory the Great around the year 600 AD, which modified the monument of Constantine to the Apostle, and the second altar was built by Pope Callistus II in 1123 AD. The present altar consists of a single block of Greek marble from the Forum of Nerva. It was consecrated by Pope Clement VIII in 1594. Seven steps lead up to the altar, and only the pope or a specified delegate may celebrate Mass on the altar.

# 79 Above the Altar, a bronze artwork resembles a canopy of cloth

Bernini's splendid bronze canopy adorns the Altar of the Confession. The canopy—properly called a *baldacchino*—has a cover that resembles the draping cloth, fringes, and tassles of a movable canopy. Although frozen in bronze, it appears to be in movement, almost swayed by a breeze.

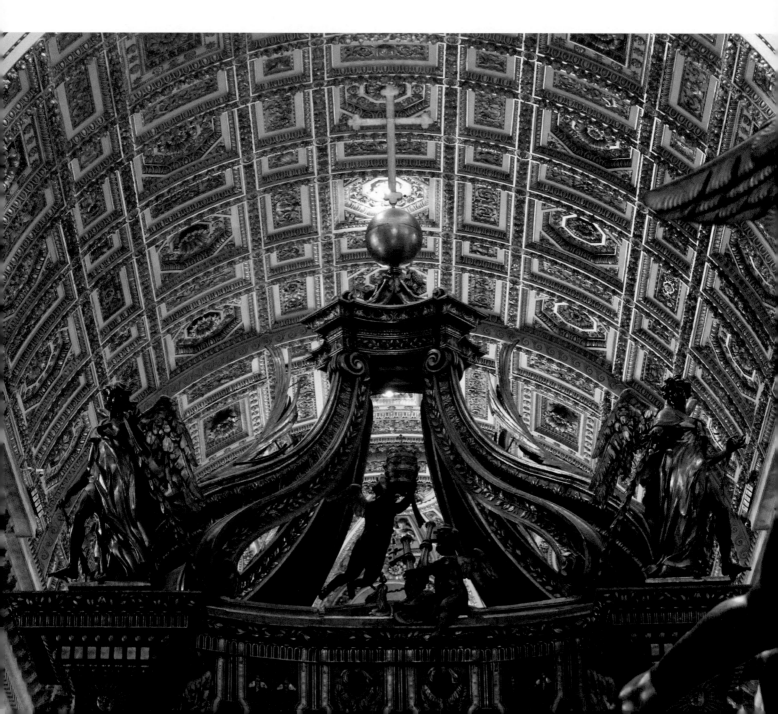

# Bernini's canopy honors St. Peter as a martyr

Since ancient times, canopies have been placed over altars with the mortal remains of a martyr. The word martyr means "witness," and those who died for the Faith were seen as chosen participants in a unique blood relationship with Christ. Bernini's *Baldacchino* honors St. Peter, the chief martyr of the early Church.

*"Behold, a great multitude which no man could number, from every nation, from all tribes and peoples and tongues, standing before the throne and before the Lamb, clothed in white robes, with palm branches in their hands, and crying out in a loud voice, 'Salvation belongs to our God who sits upon the throne, and to the Lamb.'"*

REVELATION 7:9–10

# 81

# A baldacchino is meant to suggest a bridal chamber

The Canopy has an etymology of "a bed with netting" and baldacchino comes from a word for "silk cloth" with the implication of bed covering. Just as a husband and wife might close the curtains on a canopy over their marriage bed for privacy during marital union, so Bernini's *Baldacchino* reminds us that the altar area and its surrounding sanctuary are the bridal chamber of God. The Lord invites each member of the Church, his Bride, into his bridal chamber (cf. Ephesians 5:25–27). As husband and wife become one flesh, so the person who accepts the invitation of Jesus Christ can become intimately one with God.

*"I have been crucified with Christ; it is no longer I who live, but Christ who lives in me; and the life I now live in the flesh I live by faith in the Son of God, who loved me and gave himself for me."*

—GALATIANS 2:20

# It took twenty-six years for Bernini to finish the *Baldacchino*

The work was unveiled at Vespers on the feast of St. Peter, 1633. It is 95 feet tall, almost the size of the Statue of Liberty (from the statue's heel to head). On the orders of Pope Urban VIII, a member of the Barberini family, a large part of the bronze for the canopy was stripped from the Pantheon. This move was criticized and led to the expression: "What the barbarians (barbari) did not do, the Barberini did."

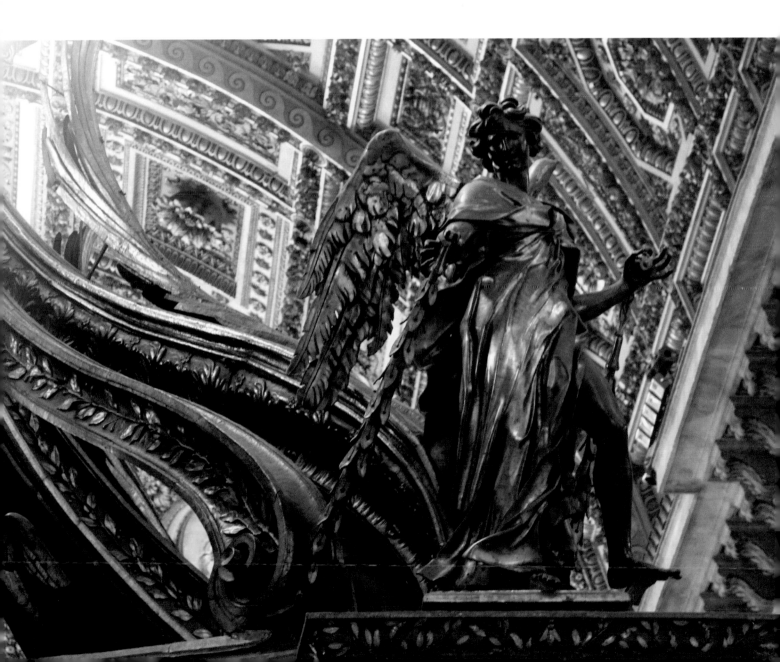

# 83 Barberini's crest depicts a woman in travail and new life

Barberini's crest is at the base of the *Baldacchino*. Above the family crest, we see a woman's face. Beginning from the southeast, right side of the canopy, and moving clockwise, the woman's face changes. At first, it appears distressed and then joyful and then restful. It concludes with the face of a baby. On the base of the columns, the natural process of the marital act is displayed and it concludes on the northeast, the left side of the canopy, with the fruition of a child. This series of images, using the natural process as a guide, shows the spiritual union between God and the person who accepts his invitation to be with him. As the natural union brings forth new life, so union with God also brings forth new life.

*"When a woman is in travail she has sorrow, because her hour has come; but when she is delivered of the child, she no longer remembers the anguish, for joy that a child is born into the world."*

—JOHN 16:21

# The canopy's columns resemble those of the Temple of Jerusalem

# 84

The canopy is supported by four columns which were modeled on older ones from the first St. Peter's Basilica. Those older columns followed the design of the Holy Column on which the Lord Jesus leaned while teaching in the Temple of Jerusalem. The columns of the canopy are divided into three parts. The first, lower part, has helicoidal fluting, typical of Roman tombs, symbolizing the soul's ascent to the afterlife. The second and third, upper parts of the columns, are decorated with gold, laurel branches and angels.

# 85

## On the ceiling of the canopy is the image of the Holy Spirit as a dove

The image fills the entire ceiling of the *Baldacchino*. It represents the sanctifying work of the Holy Spirit on the altar and in the life of the Church.

"THE SPIRIT AND THE BRIDE SAY, 'COME.'"

—REVELATION 22:17

# The massive cupola high above the *Baldacchino* contains a smaller dome

# 86

In this smaller dome—called a lantern—is an image of God the Father majestically dressed in red and is surrounded by blue. The image's location above displays the Father's omniscience. It depicts the Father lifting his hand in blessing, showing his divine providence over all.

*"Blessed be the God and Father of our Lord Jesus Christ, who has blessed us in Christ with every spiritual blessing in the heavenly places."*

—EPHESIANS 1:3

# From the lantern, to the dove, to the altar, God's saving work is displayed in the Sanctuary

## 87

God, who is Love, invites all people into a relationship with him. Here in the sanctuary of the great basilica, the dynamic and welcoming action of the Most Holy Trinity is manifested in beautiful array. The Providence of God the Father, the guidance of God the Holy Spirit, and the Altar of Sacrifice of God the Son are all shown here to believers and inquirers alike. God calls all humanity to communion with himself.

*"Now to him who by the power at work within us is able to do far more abundantly than all that we could ask or think, to him be glory in the Church and in Christ Jesus to all generations, forever and ever. Amen."*

—EPHESIANS 3:20–21

## The cupola of St. Peter's Basilica has ninety-six mosaic figures

## 88

The mosaics are highlighted by red, gold, and blue gilding. The heavenly decoration is divided by sixteen vaulting ribs that converge at the top of the dome and are separated into six horizontal fields: on the highest field, flights of seraphim are displayed; on the second field, angels reverently look down upon St. Peter's tomb; on the third field, flights of cherubim are depicted; on the fourth field, sixteen angels hold the symbols and instruments of the Passion; on the fifth field, the glorious figure of Christ is shown, surrounded by the Blessed Virgin Mary, St. John the Baptist, St. Paul, and the Twelve Apostles; and, on the lowest field, there are depictions of the first sixteen popes, all of whom are buried in the basilica. Below these images, the dome is illuminated by sixteen windows, whose natural light gives added attention to the mosaic figures.

# 89

## The dome is meant to replicate the Pantheon

The Pantheon is the ancient temple dedicated to all the false gods. It was the conscious intention of Bramante, Michelangelo, and their team of artists, to parallel the Pantheon, and to "bring the pantheon" to the tomb of St. Peter. This was an overwhelming undertaking which required extensive pillars on the four corners of the dome, and a series of twin domes, with the external dome holding the internal dome in place by a systematic control of weight and a series of detention chains. The task was completed by the Renaissance masters, who successfully "brought the Pantheon" to St. Peter's tomb, where the shadows of the false gods met the fullness of faith in the Galilean fisherman's solemn proclamation to the Lord Jesus: "You are the Christ, the Son of the living God" (Matthew 16:16).

# 90

## A space shuttle could fit within the area of the dome

The dome of St. Peter's is massive, more than 100 feet higher than the US Capitol dome in Washington, DC, which is 287.5 feet. A space shuttle, with its external rockets and fuel tank, could fit comfortably within the area of the dome.

# 91

# There is an internal walkway between the two domes

Since two domes were needed to build the massive cupola, there is a small passage between the two. Inside is a narrow spiral staircase. Visitors and pilgrims alike can ascend the steps of the cupola, walking at an incline literally between the two domes, and reach the heights of the lantern at the very top of the cupola.

# St. Peter's Basilica has a coffee bar and souvenir shop on its roof

St. Peter's might be the only church in the world that has a coffee bar and souvenir shop on its roof. As a person reaches the end of the steps to the cupola (or exits the elevator bypassing the steps), before entering the incline portion of the twin domes, there is a fully functioning coffee bar and souvenir shop. A person can boast that they had a snack and a cup of coffee, literally, on the top of St. Peter's Basilica.

"... LISTEN TO ME, AND YOU SHALL EAT WELL, YOU SHALL DELIGHT IN RICH FARE."

—ISAIAH 55:2B (NABRE)

# 93

## Around the rotundo of the dome are words of the Lord Jesus to St. Peter:

TU ES PETRUS, ET SUPER HANC PETRAM AEDIFICABO ECCLESIAM MEAM, ET PORTAE INFERI NON PRAEVALEBUNT ADVERSUS EAM.

*"And I tell you, you are Peter, and on this rock I will build my church, and the powers of death shall not prevail against it"* (Matthew 16:18).

# The Crypt of the Popes was created with the new basilica

In building the new church, the floor of the old Constantinian basilica was vaulted over in order to raise the pavement by about seven feet. This created the crypt, and about 140 popes are buried in this general area. Before his beatification, Pope John Paul II was buried here in these grottoes.

# The sepulcher of St. Peter is within these grottoes

The sepulcher of St. Peter is reached by descending a double ramp of stairs from the marble floor of the new basilica. Called the *Confessio*, in honor of St. Peter's statement of faith, the area is an enclosed balustrade and is decorated with multi-colored marble floor and walls. The sepulchral chamber is located in the central niche of this area.

# The large bronze urn contains the *pallia*—not St. Peter's bones

In the sepulchral chamber, there is a large bronze urn. Many mistakenly believe that the bones of St. Peter are located in this urn; however, in the urn are contained the pallia (the plural form of *pallium*). The pallium is a white wool vestment, worn like a yoke and embroidered with six crosses. The pallia are prepared and bestowed every year by the pope. They are worn by the pope, patriarchs, and metropolitan archbishops throughout the world. Metropolitan archbishops are those archbishops who are "in the field" shepherding an archdiocese and guiding an ecclesiastical province.

# 97 The pallia are made of wool to signify that bishops are shepherds

The yoke-shape of the vestment represents the yoke of the Lord and reminds those who receive them that they must be like the Good Shepherd, always willing to lay down their lives for their sheep. This is emphasized by the crosses on the pallia, which are symbolic of the sacred wounds of Christ.

# The pallia are woven from wool blessed on January 21, the feast of St. Agnes

## 98

The Feast Day of St. Agnes was chosen for the blessing of the pallia because Agnes means "lamb," and the saint was known to be a martyr and virgin with great purity of faith and body. Symbolizing this purity, red and white crowns are placed on the heads of the lambs as they are prepared to be blessed and sheared. Their wool is used to make the pallia. The pallia are placed in the niche the night before the feast of Saints Peter and Paul (June 29), and during the Mass on the feast day, the pope places the pallia on the shoulders of all the previous year's new metropolitan archbishops.

# 99 In the sepulchral chamber is the Lord Jesus' invitation to eternal life

Above the bronze urn is a mosaic of Jesus Christ. In the central mosaic, the Lord Jesus is giving his blessing, while holding an open Gospel book to humanity. On the book's open pages, translated, the text reads: "I am Truth and Life, those who believe in me will live on."

*"I am the way, and the truth, and the life; no one comes to the Father, but by me."*

—JOHN 14:6

# The Confessio reminds us of the Parable of the Lost Sheep

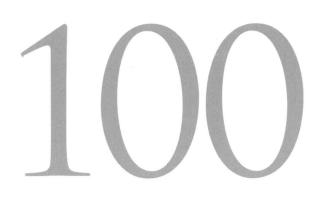

Surrounding the Confessio, there are ninety-nine candles. The number ninety-nine is traditionally associated with eternity. Within the ninety-nine candles, there are seven large candles hanging in front of the sepulchral niche. The number seven is traditionally associated with perfection. The symbolism of the numbers is important as they express the eternity and perfection of the promise offered to humanity in Jesus Christ. The number ninety-nine is also reminiscent of the parable of the lost sheep. The shepherd will leave the ninety-nine and seek out the one that has gone astray (Matthew 18:10–14). The Lord Jesus, and St. Peter as his chief Apostle, will leave the ninety-nine—represented by the candles—and seek out the one that is lost—which is each of us standing at the Confessio.

*"What do you think? If a man has a hundred sheep, and one of them has gone astray, does he not leave the ninety-nine on the hills and go in search of the one that went astray?"*

—MATTHEW 18:12

# 101 The Basilica is built on the very bones of St. Peter

St. Peter's bones were always believed to be beneath the place where the basilica now stands, but their exact location was never specifically known. They were accidentally discovered in the middle of the twentieth century, and in 1968, after decades of scientific tests, Pope Paul VI announced that the bones in question were truly those of the Apostle Peter himself.

Literally, on the bones of St. Peter the majestic basilica is built, and on this first pope, who declared to the Lord Jesus—"You are the Christ, the Son of the living God"—the Church is built.

# Image credits

Photos copyright © Justin Gaeta, Thursday Night Productions with the exception of the following:

Cover: *St. Peter's Basilica.* Sailorr / Dreamstime. 2011.

Dedication: *St. Peter's Basilica In Vatican.* maxphotography / iStock. 2012.

Foreword: *Roma Panoramica I.* Samora, Filipe. 2009.

5 *Vatican Flag.* 2013. Ciuffo, Leandro Neumann. https://www.flickr.com/people/18115835@ N00.

10 *Vatican City circa 1984.* catwalker / ShutterStock; *Vatican postage stamp ca. 1949.* hipproductions / ShutterStock; *Vintage airmail labels and stamps* Christian Mueringer / Dreamstime.

11 *Pope Francis Delivers His Urbi et Orbi Blessing.* Origlia, Franco / Stringer / Getty Images. 2013.

12 *Pope Francis coin.* A1977 / Dreamstime. 2014.

13 *BRAZIL-POPE-WYD-ARRIVAL.* AFP / Pool. 2013; *The Popemobile.* EdStock / iStock. 2014.

14 *Vatican-Pope-Audience.* Solaro, Andreas / Getty Images. 2014.

15 *Saint Peter as Pope.* Rubens, Peter Paul. 1610–1612.

18 *Crocifissione di san pietro.* Giordano, Luca. 1692.

20 *Archbasilica of St. John Lateran.* ribeiroantonio / iStock. 2014.

21 *John Paul II Stamp.* satori13 / iStock. 2014.

27 *Saint Peters Square, Rome.* Nikada / iStock. 2010.

36 *Swiss Guard Stands at an Entrance of the Vatican.* omersukrugoksu / iStock. 2014.

37 *Charlemagne Agostino Cornacchini Vatican.* Myrabella / Wikimedia Commons. 2009.

50 *Pieta (marble) (detail).* Buonarroti, Michelangelo. Bridgeman Art. 1498–1499.

58 *Tomb of St. John Paul II at St. Sebastian's Altar.* Pawlik, Wojciech / Wikimedia Commons. 2011.

59 *Interior of St Peter's in Rome.* Pannini, Giovanni Paolo / Wikimedia Commons. 1750s.

60 *St Peter's Basilica.* Osmond, James / Getty Images. 2014; *Decorations by Gian Lorenzo Bernini.* Cigolini, G. / DEA / Getty Images. 2014.

64 *Saint Veronica.* Wikimedia Commons. 2007.

67 *Vatican Altar.* Landy, Patrick / Wikimedia Commons. 2008.

70 *Bernini Masterpiece.* Pavlukovic, Bojan / ShutterStock. 2014.

77 *Saint Peter's Statue Saint Peter's Basilica Vatican City.* Jebulon / Wikimedia Commons. 2013.

95 *Detail of marble decoration from Papal altar of Confession.* Cigolini, G. / DEA / Getty Images. 2014.

97 *Deacons carry the Palliums.* Pizzoli, Alberto / Getty Images. 2008.

98 *Vatican-Pope-Mass-Pallium.* Solaro, Andreas / Getty Images. 2008.

# About the author

Fr. Jeff Kirby is a priest of the Diocese of Charleston. He holds a Licentiate in Moral Theology from the Holy Cross University in Rome. As the diocesan Vicar of Vocations, Fr. Kirby has guided numerous young men and women in the spiritual life and in the process of discernment. In 2011, he founded the Drexel House, a Catholic Residence for men.

---

# Saint Benedict Press

Saint Benedict Press publishes books, Bibles, and multimedia that explore and defend the Catholic intellectual tradition. Our mission is to present the truths of the Catholic faith in an attractive and accessible manner.

Founded in 2006, our name pays homage to the guiding influence of the Rule of Saint Benedict and the Benedictine monks of Belmont Abbey, just a short distance from our headquarters in Charlotte, NC.

Saint Benedict Press publishes under several imprints. Our TAN Books imprint (TANBooks.com), publishes over 500 titles in theology, spirituality, devotions, Church doctrine, history, and the Lives of the Saints. Our Catholic Courses imprint (CatholicCourses.com) publishes audio and video lectures from the world's best professors in Theology, Philosophy, Scripture, Literature and more.

**For a free catalog, visit us online at**
**TANBooks.com**

**Or call us toll-free at**
**(800) 437-5876**